Contents

BIDEFORD
Appledore,
Instow &
Westward Ho!

© Rosemary Lauder 1996

ISBN 0-9528645-0-9

Printed by Maslands, Tiverton

Published 1996

North Devon Books, Bideford

An early view of the first Appledore quay

There **is an indefinable air of romance** about an estuary. The broad placid waters of the adult river are about to merge with the vast mass of the ocean. From the safe, familiar haven of his home port, the sailor on board his ship slips downstream, between the treelined banks and friendly villages, known to him from his boyhood. The flow of the current carries him more swiftly and the salt tang gets stronger. Suddenly the land falls away and there it is – the limitless horizon – the ceaseless movement of the waves, the white breakers proclaiming the presence of the Bar, the final barrier before the open sea is reached.

And beyond lies – what? The very frailty of a ship upon the restless, tossing sea has always brought a sense of wonder to the onlookers. What folly to trust men's lives to a few planks of wood, all that keeps them afloat above unfathomable depths. Untameable and unpredictable, its magic and mystery will always fascinate and lure those who live within sight and sound of the sea.

The estuary of the Torridge is impressive. Two major rivers join together within a mile of the open sea. The Taw is fed from the soggy mass of Dartmoor many miles to the south, and the Torridge, with its birth place less than 20 miles away on the Cornish border, loops and twists for over 50 miles before reaching the home straight above Bideford. The land has one last barrier to block the sailor's free passage, and one last hurdle barring the returning ship from the safety of calm waters. Across the mouth of the estuary is the fearsome sand Bar that over the centuries has claimed innumerable lives, and still today is a major hazard, passable only towards High water. Even on calm and windless days, there is a restlessness, an uneasy churning of the waters that is marked with white foam. Rough weather brings huge breakers crashing on the Bar, and the change in movement as you sail out to the open sea is immediate and very distinct.

For all its breadth and strong tidal flow, there is only one narrow passage that is safely navigable by larger vessels. Strangers to the estuary are guided by a pilot boat, and such is the nature of the shifting sands that the river Taw is no longer accessible to anything but small craft and sand dredgers.

The Torridge estuary has always been a busy place. Today it is in decline, with little or no evidence of the teeming maritime industry that once cluttered its banks, when sailors and fishing folk, boat builders and sailmakers, congregated together in Appledore, and Bideford was the second most important port in the land. History has come and gone. The Danes sailed up the tidal waters in their bloody raiding parties; the travelling missionaries waded across the dangerous swirling currents to take their message to the isolated hamlets. Traders also diced with death as they were rowed across, until in the 13th century the first bridge was built at Bideford – with a chapel of thanksgiving (and for the collection of alms) at either end, and in the middle, just in case.

Bideford and Appledore grew in importance. The gentry built themselves town houses, and Bideford quay was a bustling, thriving place. From here Sir Richard Grenville and his men set sail for New England, and returned, their holds laden with booty, and the tales of all they had seen and done must have held the townsfolk spellbound. Again, in 1591, they set off to fight for their Queen, waylaying the Spanish treasure fleet off the Azores – Sir Richard's last voyage from which neither he, nor his men, nor his ship, returned. The gallant little *Revenge* became isolated from the rest of the English ships and withstood an onslaught from several much larger Spanish galleons for 15 hours before Sir Richard, mortally wounded, and to save the lives of his crew, surrendered, much against his own wishes. He died shortly afterwards, and the *Revenge* and all on board perished in a sudden storm a few days later, together with many of their Spanish adversaries.

When all had settled down once more, trade grew and grew with the New World across the Atlantic, and Bideford, with a new quay to match its now superior trading position, became a place of broad streets and large houses, of warehouses, and customs officials, and all seemed safe and secure. In Appledore the fishing folk were kept busy, and they in turn gave plenty of work to all the various trades and crafts associated with the sea.

Gradually trade declined and by the end of the 18th century Bideford's long slide had begun. But the estuary has not given up without a fight, and there remains one large shipyard, a flagship for North Devon, and still there are men who keep alive the old traditions and crafts. The banks of the Torridge are lined with disused quays and wharves and wooden hulks rotting out below the tide line, but whilst the tide flows in and out twice a day, and whilst salt tangs the air, the estuary will be home to those with the sea in their veins to whom the water is a way of life. Old salts truly never give up!

Appledore has seen several changes over the centuries, with the development of a very early dry dock, the realignment of the quay wall at least twice, and the disappearance from the scene of the multitude of small boatyards, sail lofts etc. of which much evidence still remains. Today many of the small cottages are holiday homes, and only the mighty Appledore Shipyard keeps alive the ancient tradition.

There are two separate communities at Appledore, and although the church and modern carpark occupy what was once marshland and a slip between East and West Appledore, they remain separate. West Appledore has no quay and here the small cottages still back on to the shore as they once did all along the estuary, but without

gardens sloping down to the foreshore. Some, in fact, appear to almost overhang the water. The narrow streets and small courtyards, all of which were originally cobbled, are a constant source of surprise and wonderment to visitors. The presence of double yellow lines would seem to be entirely superfluous!

The Church is comparatively modern, 1837, but is worth a visit for its maritime flavour. The pulpit rises from a stone coil of rope and there are many monuments to the seafaring community both around the walls and in the graveyard outside.

East Appledore is the larger community, its steep streets climbing in straight lines up the hillside, the houses becoming larger and more prosperous the higher you get, and it is here almost on the summit that the wealthy shipowners and builders had their houses.

Many of the cottages are now owned by folk from away, but before remarks about 'second homes' are uttered, it must be said that many of these 'quaint' cottages are small and inconvenient, without back gardens or sometimes even yards, nowhere to park the car, nowhere for the kids to play, and not really the place for a 20th century housewife. She prefers her roomy, healthier, centrally heated house on the hill, and the only reason most of these cottages escaped the wholesale slum clearances that ripped the heart out of Bideford in the 1970s is that it would have meant pulling down most of old Appledore.

At least the holiday folk keep the cottages in good repair and bring trade for much of the year to the local shops and pubs, although Appledore can be a quiet place in the winter months.

The oldest properties are along Market Street; most of those that front the quay date from after its construction in the 1840s, built on the made up ground formed when the new quay was built on what were the gardens and slips of the Market Street properties.

In time it was realised that this quay wall was crumbling badly and that in places the infill had disappeared completely. Despite the wartime economies, Appledore's new quay was completed in 1939, doubling the width of the frontage, and this area has been little changed since.

There are many quaint and hidden corners in

both East and West Appledore, and it was certainly never planned with the motor car in mind. Many of the cottages have interesting architectural features and as most of it is now a conservation area, there are no plastic replacements or unsightly modern windows to mar the charm.

If Old Salts go to heaven, then they must be looking down in despairing disbelief on Appledore. Only a century or so ago they would have recognised their old hometown – the noisy quay, the narrow courts and opes and drangs, all full of the salt-encrusted paraphernalia of

Market Street

fishermen and boat builders. All along the quay, craft of all shapes and sizes would have been tied up, waiting for the tide, or a cargo. Outside and inside the numerous alehouses, the seafaring community would have congregated. Almost everyone owed their livelihood to the sea – if you didn't then there was little point in living at Appledore. Those who didn't put to sea built and repaired vessels for others to sail.

At one time Appledore could boast its own merchant fleet, engaged in the profitable coastal trade, as well as the more everyday business of fishing. The village also had many shipyards from the very smallest to the mighty Richmond Dry dock, completed in 1856 and in its day a splendid innovation, being one of the very first dry docks to be built.

So what happened to it all? The small yards and traditional skills had been linked to the age of sail. But once that went, replaced first by the age of steam, and then by the roads, they were doomed. A few survived almost until the present day building small wooden boats and yachts, but the grand era had gone – down the river with the ebb tide.

The Richmond Dry Dock proved to be a lifeline and ship building, or at least repairing, has been more or less continuous. There have been peaks and troughs; work had all but dried up when the Second World War brought a demand for new ships, and the momentum carried on with the yard

Appledore waterfront prior to the construction of the covered yard

*The Pulpit,
St Mary's
Appledore*

producing a great variety of fine vessels. But shipbuilding has .always been a chancy business and Appledore has had its share of failures.

In 1963 the yard was declared bankrupt throwing 300 men out of work overnight. Such was the concern locally that a consortium of local businessmen formed Appledore Shipbuilders to take over the yard and carry on the tradition. It survived, and its future seemed assured when Europe's largest covered shipyard began to take shape, and was completed in 1970.

A wide variety of vessels have been completed by the yard – and there have been some unusual projects. The skyline was somewhat altered when a drilling platform floated up the estuary to be shortened. Great interest was aroused when the coastline off Westward Ho! acquired a temporary 'wreck'. One of the huge Newport dock gates being towed to the yard for repair work unfortunately decided to come to rest a few miles out to sea. Various methods were attempted to refloat her, all watched with great interest, and eventually she was recovered and completed her journey up the estuary. The yard is much used by the RNLI – but the shipbuilding trade is as vulnerable as it ever was. Twice the shipyard has almost foundered, and despite being taken over by the government in 1974, its future is as uncertain today as at any period in its history. If it should close, then the estuary will have lost its last link with a great shipbuilding history.

Already the once famous yard that reconstructed the *Golden Hind* and *Nonsuch* is fading from memory. In solitary splendour, beyond the lifeboat slip, it lies empty and abandoned, its corrugated covering loosening with the winds of winter – awaiting only a fierce gale to complete its downfall. It was in 1968 that the little yard of Hinks & Son, which had been building ships for three generations, shot to fame when they were commissioned to build the replica of the *Nonsuch* to celebrate the three hundredth anniversary of the founding of the Hudson Bay Company in northern Canada. At Hinks' yard and in Appledore many of the age-old skills required for such an ambitious and imaginative project still existed, and many a retired Appledore man found himself once again called upon to practise a craft he had thought would never again be needed. Great interest and pride was generated, and when she was launched in August 1968, the river banks were packed, and anyone who had a boat – or anything that would float – was out there to watch. She was to have crossed the Atlantic under her own power (an engine, the only modern note, had been installed for this purpose) but her owners decided not to risk it after she had been rescued by the Lizard lifeboat, a victim of heavy seas and gale force winds.

Four years later the *Golden Hind* left Hinks' yard. She was twice the size of the Nonsuch and the yard had to be extended, with a special viewing gallery so that the public could watch the fascinating work in progress. This time, with a local crew, she completed the voyage across the Atlantic to her San Franciscan home, and has proved her worth by being almost continuously at sea, and she was used in the filming of *Shogun* in Japan. These two beautiful galleons were followed by a Viking longship and a Roman galley.

The Maritime Museum in Odun Road houses a fascinating collection and explores the past history of Appledore and the estuary. The full story is told in 'Appledore – Handmaid of the Sea' by John Beara.

The 'Nonsuch'

An early view of Instow and the Estuary. Instow railway station is in the foreground.

Instow developed in an entirely different manner to Appledore, and although they stare at each other across the water and a ferry plies to and fro, the folk are as different as chalk and cheese. A river is commonly a division – a boundary – between parishes, counties and countries. The people who live along the banks often have little or nothing in common with their (literally) opposite numbers and are all too often at enmity, or at least at odds with them. Appledore children went barefoot and often hungry, their mothers hitched up their skirts and gathered laver from the rocks at low tide; their dads drank in the numerous ale houses, swore at their families, and put to sea in the early dawn to catch fish that none might starve.

Instow's inhabitants were more likely to be retired colonials, or ex military and naval officers looking for reasonable accommodation on a restricted pension. The children went to private academies, and the list of residents was sprinkled with titles, colonels, captains and doctors.

Yet Instow's beginnings were much the same as Appledore's. There were two small settlements of fisherfolk, one at either end of the present-day Instow, and unconnected except by a riverside path.

Around 1610 the Quay was built and Instow began to expand as its popularity as a small port grew, especially with the Barnstaple merchants as it saved negotiating the difficult channels of the Taw. It was one of the earliest properly constructed quays on the estuary – and the only one to be built jetty-fashion to enable ships of some size to come alongside. A sizeable maritime settlement developed around the quay and the trade continued until the early part of the 18th century. The cottages and warehouses of this time

Cottages at Lane End

were further back than the line of the terrace that today fronts the estuary. This was not built until the seawall was constructed, and the houses form a frontage to the original much older dwellings that now form the 'back quarters'.

At the far end were a collection of cottages, built in the traditional cramped style as if folk were afraid to spread out and needed the comfort of each other for warmth and protection. Here was the original pub and village lock-up, several shops, and the lane that went up to the 12th century church, and on up the hill to join the road that ran over the high ground between Bideford and Barnstaple.

Instow's gentrification began in the Victorian age when it was fashionable for a family to retire to the seaside for the summer months. But Instow decided to go one better than become a mere seaside resort – it was to be a spa, no less, and was developed almost in one go. It would seem that Instow enjoyed a boom period in the late 1830s when many of the terraces, villas and larger houses

were built. It must have looked very grand and somewhat strange to the cluttered fishing village across the water! No doubt the grand folk, promenading after dinner in their evening dress, liked to gaze across and proclaim how quaint it all was. Come to think of it, they still do!

The inhabitants of Instow were used to a social life, and to belonging to clubs. The North Devon Lawn Tennis and Croquet Club flourished for many years at Lane End, although it was somewhat exclusive. The lady in the picture, one of the instigators and leading lights of the club, was Miss Hinchliff, who designed the clubhouse.

After the closure of the club in 1954, the land was sold and has now been built on. The thatched clubhouse stood for many years, converted into a bungalow, but that, too has disappeared and been replaced by a modern house.

Equally exclusive was the North Devon Yacht Club, first formed in 1905. It was originally known as the Taw and Torridge Yacht Club and catered for visitors as well as the local gentry. Until 1972 its headquarters were the house on the jetty, now over-shadowed by the new flats, and for many years it was equally popular as a social gentlemen's club with almost as many bridge-playing members as sailors.

Although its original home was prestigious, the new premises are more spacious and convenient: in 1972 the yacht club took over the defunct Instow railway station, converted the buildings to changing rooms and built themselves a new clubhouse.

Visitors are welcome, particularly at the various Open Weeks held throughout the summer and at the annual Regatta in August.

The cricket club is older than either the tennis or yacht clubs, and is one of the oldest in the country. The North Devon Cricket Club was formed in Barnstaple in 1823 and moved to its

The North Devon Lawn Tennis & Croquet Club

present site in 1832. Cricket is played in all sorts of strange places and odd corners but there can be few pitches anywhere in the world as beautifully situated as Instow's. White figures on a perfect greensward backed by the blue of the sea on a summer's afternoon – could there be a more English scene? The thatched clubhouse was originally a barn, old even when the cricketers first moved in.

The advertisement that appeared in June, 1838 in the local North Devon Advertiser and Weekly Chronicle gives a fascinating glimpse of Instow at that time and was obviously aimed at attracting the wealthy and the well-bred to the new resort.

BATHS AT INSTOW

WILLIAM GOAMAN

respectfully announces that he has taken the NEWLY ERECTED BATHS at Instow, which are replete with every convenience for SEAWATER, HOT, COLD and SHOWER BATHING: and attached to them are neat and comfortable FURNISHED LODGINGS.

'This delightful watering-place has, in the last year, had several new and elegant VILLAS erected in its fertile valley, which are screened through the winter months by a range of lofty hills. The sea-wall lately built has allowed the formation of a level road, thirty feet wide, in front of the Baths and Villas, presenting a ten-feet gravel promenade, half a mile in length, in addition to the unusually capacious, level and dry sands, so justly admired by every visitor.

Instow is also delightfully situated on the conflux of the Taw and Torridge rivers, opposite the Bar, having Northam, East and West Appledore, and the beautiful undulating country which surrounds it, imparting a wildness which is strongly contrasted by the numberless detached villas studded by the hand of art over its surface. In addition to this picturesque landscape, the views presented by the Bar – the island of Lundy – the vast expanse of the Atlantic Ocean – the influx and efflux of the tides – numerous pleasure, fishing and passage boats, and the transit in and out of the extensive shipping from the ports of Barnstaple and Bideford, produce new and ever-varying features, by which the eye is at all times pleasingly gratified, without fatigue. To these and other multitudinous advantages, it may be added that four mail coaches, with numberless other stage coaches and carriages pass daily through Instow, to and from the very superior market towns of Barnstaple and Bideford – from the former of which it is distant five, from the latter three miles; and the Torridge steam packet lands passengers here on its voyages to and from Bristol and Bideford weekly.

A beautifully CHALYBEATE SPRING has also been discovered in a field close by, on which its spirited proprietor intends shortly to erect a neat pump-room with appropriate walks to it. This, and the completion, of the other numerous residences designed for erection, will lead the contented and reflecting mind to exclaim, the consummation of all earthly wishes may be imagined in this favoured spot, already proved by its visitors, and admitted by the Faculty, to be the most healthy and therefore best adapted residence for the prolongation of life.'

Instow, June 13, 1838

Sadly the 'spirited proprietor' never built his pump room and the Torridge steam packet has long since ceased to ply up and down the estuary. The mail and stage coaches too have disappeared from the scene, and the Trade Description Act would frown on the claim that Instow embodies the 'consummation of all earthly wishes'.

In 1801 Instow had a population of 347. By 1871 this had almost doubled to 647 living, according to a directory of the time, in 127 houses. The same directory lists the principal residents which included a good proportion of retired naval and military officers and genteel single ladies. It tells us the occupations of those less fortunately placed, which included a tailor, horse dealer, mastermariner, 2 bootmakers, grocer, postmaster, 2 butchers, land agent, dressmakers, blacksmith, victualler, builder, livery stable, beerhouse, a ladies boarding and day school and 16 lodging houses.

Before the road along the front was built, when Instow consisted of two small, separate communities, each was largely self-supporting.

Lane End had its own pub, butchers shop, dairy and bakery. The Quay area and the cottages in Marsh Lane also had a butchers, a grocers and bakers, and one of the old, original cottages in a lane off the Quay, was another pub or beer-house.

The village hall, Jubilee Hall, was at Lane End and is now the Lobster Pot.

The premier hotel, Instow's 'centrepiece' was the now-demolished Marine Hotel. In its superb water's edge position it was a favourite with locals and holidaymakers. In recent years the Commodore Hotel has taken over its role, joined

Appledore viewed from across the Skern

A cricket match in progress at Instow

From an early guide book

Unlike many Devon towns and villages, the war had a tremendous impact on Instow. The long sandy beaches with their backing of sand hills were seized upon as the ideal training ground for an invasion force. Scenes soon to be enacted for real on the beaches of Northern France were first rehearsed on the hitherto peaceful and sleepy shores of the estuary.

The entire beach, sand-dunes and 'front' were placed out of bounds to the local population. The Marine Hotel and many of the large houses were taken over by the troops. The cricket pavilion became part of the REME establishment and both the Jubilee Hall and the Rifle Hall saw service as NAAFIs.

Instow soon assumed an important role as a centre for amphibious warfare, for which it was ideally suited. Tanks and landing craft became commonplace and strange structures took shape on the beach which turned out to be Bailey Bridges.

To defend all this military activity, Instow was guarded with an impressive array of concrete pill boxes, concrete gun and searchlight emplacements, roadblocks and barricades. Many of these can still be seen, as can the jagged concrete pillars in the water that defended the Quay.

Such was its value during the War that the Ministry of Defence decided to continue to make use of the estuary and its sand. Beyond the cricket pitch is now the headquarters of the 'Amphibious Trials and Training Unit Royal Marines'. To add to

by a new pub, The Quay.

The two old inns were called the Commercial and the Sailors, or Sailors Rest, which closed down when the brewery transferred its licence to the newly-built Wayfarer or New Inn at the turn of the century.

For nearly seventy years this was run by the Jordan family: Harold Jordan's mother and father moved in in 1907 and he and his wife moved out in 1973. He remembered when a bottle of whisky was 12s 6d and sixpence would buy a pint of beer and an ounce of tobacco. Full board, which included breakfast, hot lunch, tea and dinner, cost 2½ guineas per week. It seems hard to believe that these prices remained stable for years – until the outbreak of the second World War; and prior to Lloyd George's Licensing Act of 1917 pubs were open from seven in the morning until at least ten at night in those far-off halcyon days!

the many and varied activities that visitors can watch from Instow – sailing, water ski-ing, wind sailing, sand extraction, shipping, helicopter and jet flights – can be added one not usually associated with holiday resorts – amphibious training.

Nor did Instow entirely escape enemy action. On 15th August, 1940, five bombs fell directly on the village, fortunately in the sand dunes and Lane End area. All the windows of the New Inn were shattered and slates fell off the roof. The landlord recalls that for once, instead of enjoying a chat outside the pub, his customers had gone straight home. As it was no-one was killed and very little damage done.

The 'new road' to Bideford was begun in 1828, following the line of the river. In many places the marshy land and tidal inlets caused problems so that the construction was by no means easy. But at last it was completed, and must have revolutionised life for the people of Instow. Of even greater impact was the coming of the railway in 1855. The London and South Western branch line from Barnstaple and Bideford, and later on to Torrington and Okehampton, was opened in October and

The L. & S.W. Railway signal box

throughout the 'season' the arrival of each train was eagerly awaited by a gang of menfolk ready with handcarts to carry the immense amount of luggage indispensable to Victorian and Edwardian comfort. Some of the passengers were bound for Appledore, but most were taken to the hotels and boarding houses with which Instow now abounded.

The signal box alongside the level crossing at the Bideford end of Instow is now a listed building, although at one time its survival seemed uncertain. Built in 1861 and fitted with a frame of 16 levers by Stevens & Co. together with a level crossing gate, the box was closed in 1979. BR removed all the equipment and a year later vandals stripped the lead from the roof. Despite numerous offers to purchase, BR remained indifferent to its fate until it became officially recognised and 'listed'. Fortunately it lasted long enough to become a much appreciated feature of the Tarka Trail footpath.

The railway line closed at last in 1982. Passengers had ceased in 1966 but it lingered on for a while carrying freight and the occasional special down from Paddington, jammed full of enthusiasts mourning the good old days of steam. But after slumbering for a decade whilst the undergrowth took hold and the lines rusted, the era of long distance footpaths and cycle routes was upon us, and the line has gained a new lease of life as the Tarka Trail. The sleepers disappeared, the gravel vanished, the embankments were tamed – and overnight hordes of cyclists, joggers, walkers, and the occasional naturalist, discovered the delights of what must once have been a most scenic route. So popular has it become that mere walkers are advised to avoid weekends, and to keep eyes in the backs of their heads for silent cyclists approaching at speed without the friendly warning of an old-fashioned bell. The trail follows the Torridge all the way to Torrington, and on to Petersmarland where the old clay works are still going strong.

The view from Tapeley Park

Tapeley Park

Still **visible on top of the hill** in front of Tapeley Park is the base of the memorial to the last male Cleveland, killed in the Crimean War in 1854. The monument must have been an impressive landmark for it was a granite column some 50 feet in height.

Young Archibald Cleveland, the only son and heir, departed to fight for his country at the age of 21. He survived the historic Charge of the Light Brigade – a bullet was deflected by a metal accoutrement – only to be killed a few days later at the battle of Inkerman. The monument was

The gardens at Tapeley Park

erected in 1856. His sword, helmet and other possessions are on display at Tapeley Park.

The obelisk was destroyed during a tremendous thunderstorm in June 1932. A newspaper report of the time stated that blocks of granite were hurled 100 feet and the iron railings surrounding the monument were twisted.

It was a sister of the tragic Archibald who married into the Christie family and their descendants have lived at Tapeley ever since.

The elegant red brick and stone house that visitors see as they reach the end of the long drive has suffered two major face lifts. The original William & Mary house was of cob, white painted and with plain, almost severe fronts. In the 1850s a new brick facade was added with white brick stringing and, from an old picture, looked more like a public hospital or institutional building.

Present day Tapeley owes its appearance to Lady Rosamund Christie, grandmother of the present owner. From 1890 onwards she embarked on a series of improvements, including the addition of the porticos, that have greatly enhanced the house. She was also responsible for much of the internal refurbishing, carried out by John Belcher.

Tapeley is rich in plaster moulding and there are several fine ceilings, the work of Italian craftsmen. The interior of the house is a series of attractive rooms round a central hall, including a music room and a particularly ornate dining room. It boasts a fine collection of china and porcelain and contains several William Morris cabinets.

It is somewhat curious that Lady Rosamund, herself un-related to the Cleveland family, should have chosen to emphasise their ownership of Tapeley rather than that of the Christies. So strong was her feeling for them that the plaque on the house wall commemorating the alterations describes Tapeley as the 'home of the Clevelands', and it is their crest, not that of the Christies, that appears on some of the interior plasterwork.

Perhaps she had a premonition of the future for sadly this woman who did so much to enhance Tapeley had to fight a long and bitter law suit at the end of her life to retain possession of her home.

After enduring an unhappy marriage to a husband who suffered periods of insanity, she found he had willed Tapeley to a distant Cleveland relative. She and her lawyers proved his mental condition and the will was overturned.

Her only son, John Christie, seems never to have cared much for Tapeley. Instead he preferred the Christie home sheltering under the South Downs – Glyndebourne. After many struggles and ups and downs, Glyndebourne is now a byword amongst opera lovers the world over. Inevitably it is with Glyndebourne that the Christie name is linked and Tapeley has slid into second place.

The house is open for guided tours, but the gardens and grounds are open almost daily. These are well worth a visit, and are one of the major gardens of the county. They were laid out in the main in the early part of this century and are now pleasantly mature. In early spring, the long drive climbing from the Italianate lodge on the main road, is a mass of daffodils. From the plateau in front of the house the view is impressive, with the estuary of the Taw and Torridge, Appledore and Instow, and the broad expanse of Bideford Bay beyond, laid out as if from the air. Few places can better this panoramic view of the North Devon coast.

Away from the biting winds, on the sheltered sides of the house, grow many rare and luxuriant plants. A warm microclimate has enabled the terrace walls to become home to a variety of plants that do not usually grow out of doors in this country, some of which have reached amazing proportions. The terraces known as the Italian gardens were laid out by Lady Rosamund and John

Belcher with the help of a local architect, Mr H. Orfoot. Together they created a most memorable garden. The lower lawn was at one time divided into eight herbaceous borders, each over 60 feet long and protected by a bay hedge. But lack of staff and maintenance costs caused their demise and they were grassed over. The curious tunnel formed of the evergreen, or 'holm' oak, survives at one end, as does the lily pond at the other. Here, and on the upper borders, major replanting has recently been undertaken which will bring new life to the gardens. A long flight of steps formed of war-surplus headstones, leads up to the highest point where huge pine trees withstand the elements, and the icehouse and shell house are to be found, on the way to the kitchen gardens.

A woodland walk to the north is one of the older parts of the garden. A broad track leads down through oak and beech trees, between banks of rhododendrons and camellias, and a plentiful smothering of primroses, to the valley where the stream has been dammed to form two small lakes. Here huge, towering evergreens, mainly cypresses, are mirrored in the water and a white marble memorial commemorates Augustus Clevland who 'made this place' in 1841, and died in 1849.

Instow and the Christie family

The present day appearance of Instow and its restrained character owe much to the Christie family. The Estate owns a large proportion of Instow and most of the agricultural land surrounding it centred on Tapeley Park.

The policy of the Christie Estate does not permit any caravans or camping or holiday development. Visitors to Instow will search in vain for bingo halls, ice-cream parlours or amusement arcades. If it were not for this strict policy, what would Instow look like today? Instead of being surrounded by pleasant farmland, would there be acres of chalets and rows of caravans? The terraces along the front, which give Instow so much of its character, would be 'fun spots' with flashing lights and non-stop blaring music – and I would not be writing this book and in all probability you would not have even bothered to visit the place.

Property owned by the Estate is, at the time of writing, painted in cream and dark green so it is easy to spot which houses in a terrace have been sold off!

The Estate also own the sand-dunes, the cricket pitch, the jetty – and that golden foreshore on which so many people spend many happy hours, quite ignorant of the fact that they do so by courtesy of the Christie Estate.

Back in 1855 the Estate took advantage of the opportunity given to them by the Crown to purchase their 'sea frontage'. With the exception of two narrow strips they now own the entire foreshore from the cricket pitch almost as far as Bideford Bridge.

Development in Instow has been restrained, and in appearance it has altered little since the major building of the 19th century. The most recent addition is the new sea wall built as part of the flood defences of the estuary in 1993. It is generally approved of because although most North Devonians are resistant to change of any kind, flood water as a regular feature of winter conditions is not a pleasant fact of life. Sandbags still make their appearance at front doors when high tides are forecast, but this is more out of habit than necessity.

The shifting sands that blow from the beach on to the road and into the gardens of the houses along the front was the reason for another change. The repaired sea wall and sophisticated road barriers do not do anything to prevent the sand blocking the road – they merely make it easier to shut it off to cars, in the same way that snow barriers operate on main roads up north.

Newish blocks of flats have replaced the old Marine Hotel, and been built on what was marshland between the quay and the railway line, and new housing is tucked away at the far end of the village.

Most of the surrounding land is still owned by the Christie estate and so far this side of the estuary has been spared the awful rash of piecemeal development that so disfigures the southern bank as one field after another is sold off for building.

To a modern generation used to civilisation at the flick of a switch it may come as a shock to realise that a century ago there were no such things as 'mains'. In Instow there was no water supply until 1910 – all those hotels and guesthouses relied on wells and hand-pumped supplies. Gas came after the first World War, and electricity not until the 1930s.

And later in the twentieth century came the biggest single change in the entire history of the estuary – the coming of the New Bridge.

The working jetty in use to construct the piers

The Torridge Bridge

A **replacement for Bideford's historic bridge** had been discussed for almost as long as anybody could remember. Firm proposals began to take shape in 1972; in 1976 a preferred route was announced and after much for-ing and against-ing, was decided upon – a high level structure flying across the estuary, downstream from Bideford and providing an effective by-pass. This, it transpired, was part of the new link road connecting North Devon to the M5.

Work began in the late autumn of 1984, and the bridge itself was completed by December, 1986. Crowds flocked to see this amazing feat of twentieth century engineering on its official opening in May 1987.

The Torridge Bride is a graceful structure, soaring high above the waters of the Torridge, one of the largest bridges to be built this century. Yet undeniably it has ruined the tranquility of the estuary. Wherever you go, the noise of the traffic is ever present.

The following is taken from *Torridge Bridge and Bideford By-Pass* by Sandra Yeo, published in 1987 by Badger Books of Bideford:

"The first construction that took shape across the river was the 240 metre working pier, which some people thought was the bridge itself. Tubular steel piles were steam-hammered into the river bed, then longitudinal steel beams were run along the top of each row of piles. Spanned by abutting concrete slabs, precast on site and simply dropped into position. It was fortunate that the deep water channel of the river runs to the east, because this had to be kept open, and had this not been the case, the jetty would have had to come out from the Westleigh side, right away from the main roadworks and the casting shed would have had to be set up that side, temporarily despoiling even more farmland.

The bridge is 650m long and 13.3m wide. A headroom of 24m above high water is provided to enable commercial shipping to continue to use the quay at Bideford.

The superstructure is an eight span prestressed concrete box made up of 251 segments. The heaviest of these are the pierhead sections weighing 105 tonnes, down to 55 tonnes for a mid-span segment, and each is a single cell box with cantilever wings. All 251 were cast at Heywood Road at the Shed, nicknamed the 'Pleasure Dome', and great was the wonderment when these sections suddenly began to line up like giant lego bricks either side of the road. Apart from an initial hiccup with the first pierhead section which had to be discarded because of segregation of the concrete, the segments were churned out on a regular basis up to a rate of one a day, but it was by no means a simple process. Starting with the pierhead sections, which were cast outside the Shed, each segment had to be match-cast, that is one day's segment moved forward to form the front of the mould for the next day's segment, no two of which are geometrically the same. It is apparently impossible to produce a perfectly constructed unit, so a computer monitored each one as it was cast, in order to correct the profile with the next unit. In this way the bridge's deck profile was returned with each new segment to its theoretical outline.

Important work was going on in the old Richmond Dockyard at Appledore. The piers that take the superstructure – seven in all, plus an eastern and western abutment – include four actually in the river bed. Reading west to east, piers 2 and 5 were constructed using cofferdams, but this method for midstream piers 3 and 4 would have involved the formation of artificial islands. Therefore, the availability of the dockyard was a godsend, for it proved large enough to accept the construction of the two 650 tonne cellular

The second caisson, lopsided before settling correctly. The working jetty is alongside, and Bideford Shipyard, now a housing estate, to the left

Piers and caissons in place, the launching girder completes the spans

caisson starter bases for these two piers, a form of construction adopted by Nuttalls on an earlier contract.

It is one thing to construct main foundations of a project in relative ease away from the site, but quite another to transport them to where they belong. How do you move a 650 tonne lump of concrete up river almost two miles? The answer is you float them. First the eight cells were blanked off and compressed air injected, then steel panels were bolted on to raise the walls, thus allowing the caisson to be floated out and towed upstream.

On the first spring tide of February, 1985, and very early in the morning, the first starter section was carefully inched out through the dock entrance. The compressed air gave a draught of 3.3m and a 6" clearance over the sill and the initial use of the dockside winches soon gave way to two Cardiff based tugs which, after the release of the air, gently manoeuvred the starter section on a shallow sandbank to await the next high tide. Some 10 hours later, compressed air was reapplied, but at a lower pressure, to give a draught of 3.6m,

stability now being more important than shallow draught. The tugs then towed the caisson on its hour long journey to the bridge site, where winches took over to pull it up against its guide piles alongside the finger jetty projecting from the main working jetty. The temporary jetty was no mean structure either, but suffice it to say that while the pile driving for the supports must have given some people a headache, it had to carry considerable weights. It has now been removed having completed its job, some of the concrete deck slabs going to the North Devon Yacht Club for their jetty!

Once the caisson was positioned and before sinking could start, the caisson walls were raised a further 10-12m. 'Grabbing out' by mechanical means then began in the cells and this continued until the caisson had settled (approximately 10m) into the river bed. After placing the roofing slab, an airdeck was installed and compressed air pumped in to force the water out and allow for hand excavation. The men carrying out this work were termed 'miners'. The depth eventually reached to bedrock was 24 metres below high water and 17 metres below the river bed itself. However, unlike ordinary miners, working under compressed air conditions meant that their experiences were more those of a deepsea diver, for after each shift they had a maximum of five minutes to get into a decompression chamber, in which they had to stay, going through a slow decompression cycle for anything up to three hours.

The caisson sinking operations took until late February, 1986, to complete, during which time the other foundations and piers were taking shape. It had been hoped to have the first pierhead section of the superstructure in place before Christmas 1985, but the 165 tonne launching girder, designed by Tony Gee and Partners and built on site, proved to be a difficult beast to tame. There were even fears voiced by some of the workforce that it was just not 'man enough' to handle 105 tonnes of concrete. However, after modifications, it was transformed, in the contractor's own words, into a 'pedigree champion'. Though, now it is all over it is a question of who else wants a balanced cantilever section bridge and a fully operational and proven gantry?!

The launching girder consists of twin lattice steel trusses, 4 metres apart and 115 metres long. It has four legs – A, B, 1 and 2. Leg A at the rear of the girder, and B, approximately at mid-point, are fixed legs. Legs 1 and 2 can move on rollers running on the underside of the launcher's bottom chord, and have the main function of stabilising the bridge cantilever during building, while leg A runs on tracks laid along the bridge deck during a gantry move, but is bolted down to the completed part of the bridge during segment

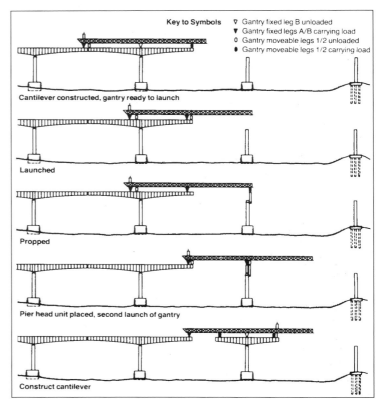

Key to Symbols
▽ Gantry fixed leg B unloaded
▼ Gantry fixed legs A/B carrying load
0 Gantry moveable legs 1/2 unloaded
● Gantry moveable legs 1/2 carrying load

Cantilever constructed, gantry ready to launch

Launched

Propped

Pier head unit placed, second launch of gantry

Construct cantilever

erection. Leg B is the main jacking support leg and is used for raising and lowering the launcher on 2 x 90 tonne rams.

The gantry moves forward on leg A, with legs B and 1 free. Leg 2 is bolted down and the gantry trusses travel across it on electrically driven chaindrive rollers. The concrete segments are supplied to the rear of the gantry by low loader and lifted by a 120 tonne 2-stage telescopic hydraulic ram mounted on a crab carriage unit. The crab assembly is powered by 4, 5.5KW motors providing direct drive to all axles. Each segment travels sideways between the lattice

The final segment moves into position

tended to want to operate against each other:– at least that is the official explanation, but mutterings amongst the work force mentioned the crab unit 'blowing up', or running over its electrical cables and short-circuiting itself!

Once the first pierhead section was finally in place in March, 1986, the real excitement, as far as the general public were concerned, began, and it was amazing how quickly the contractors made up for lost time.

Once a pierhead section was in place and temporarily stressed down, segments were applied either side using Sika glue, and, also temporarily stressed one segment to another using Dividag bars. The embryo cantilever was then checked for alignment, before the permanent bearings carried the load onto the pierhead. Once the glue had hardened between the segments, permanent strandstressing of the segments began. Rates of up to 4 segments placed per day were achieved, and consequently a 90 metre balanced cantilever was erected and stressed in 3 weeks. The mid-span closure of each newly completed section was by way of an in-situ joint. As a result of the importance of the stressing operation, separate night shifts dealt with all the strand pushing and stressing ensuring that segments could be placed during the day.

On 2nd December, 1986, with Company flag flying proudly above the crab assembly, Nuttalls placed the 251st, and final, segment of the bridge into position at the eastern abutment. The occasion, despite media attention, was surprisingly low key, and in some ways sad, as it marked the beginning of the end of this great engineering project."

and is then lowered and rotated into position. Some of the commissioning problems causing the early delay were brought about by the hydraulic systems, where the necessary safety mechanisms

From an early guide book

Bideford

Nothing could be a greater contrast than the construction methods of the two bridges! To a generation growing up reliant on massive machinery and engine power for the least little building operation, it presents an amazing lesson and monument to the skills and determination of men using nothing but their own strength and the most elementary of tools. It is extremely doubtful if there was even a plan drawn up! Only time will tell whether the new bridge will survive as Bideford Bridge has done for over six centuries, in continuous and increasing use, far more vulnerable to flood tides and carrying a volume of traffic undreamt of when it was built.

The story of Bideford is linked with the Long Bridge. The town grew up around the first possible river crossing of the estuary – By-the-Ford – which was just above the bridge by Ford House, one of the oldest houses in the town. Few today would care to wade across the muddy banks and risk themselves in the waters, which even at low tide can flow surprisingly fast. Perhaps on horse back it wasn't so bad, but it must always have been a hazardous undertaking.

The earliest bridge took shape in the fourteenth century. It was entirely of wood, and the money for it was raised by the church. The clergy were constant travellers, visiting outlying churches, collecting tythes and seeing to their farflung property, so that it was in their interests as much as anyone's to make travelling as safe as possible. There were originally supposed to have been two chapels, one at either end, presumably for the collecting of tolls to help pay for its upkeep, and it was known to have been completed by 1327. It has been widened and altered, and the piers themselves strengthened and rebuilt. Part of its charm lies in the uneven spans of the arches. Various stories account for this; one is that the surrounding parishes paid for a span each and it depended on how generous they were as to the width of the arch; another that the foundations rested on wool sacks thrown into the river to give stability, and these determined where the piers rested – or simply that as it was of wood, the length of the timber available determined the span.

Around 1500 the wooden bridge was eventually encased with stone, when the pointed arches, massive stone piers and cutwaters were built – and these are still very much in evidence, bearing the burden of modern traffic yet built in the days when horsepower had a very different meaning. The first repairs were recorded in 1638, and in 1692 the graceful sundial that forms part of the town's crest was erected. When this disappeared is not known, but a reconstruction would be a worthy addition – perhaps to mark the Bridge's retirement.

The Bridge itself is 667 feet in length, of twenty four arches varying from 12 to 25 feet on piers that also vary from 9 to 12 feet in thickness. The carriageway was originally no wider than the arches with a stone parapet projecting above the piers to allow pedestrians to make way for wheeled vehicles.

An account of the early widening of the Bridge comes from the Transactions of the Devonshire Association, 1902 written by Alexander Duncan.

In the 1700's tolls were often charged for vehicles. In 1791 instructions were issued to stop traffic that might result in injury to the structure and a chain was provided for closing off the Bridge. In 1793 the first widening was proposed. In 1795, for £295, and with a guarantee for 7 years, four of the arches were widened giving an additional two feet each side. Land at the east end was purchased to improve access and two more arches widened. In 1807 the five arches nearest the town were widened – £50 per arch. The remainder were widened in 1810 after much debate as to whether the arches could be enlarged or a drawbridge substituted.

But less than fifty years later it was again considered necessary to widen the Bridge 'in consequence of the accidents which have occurred by its narrowness' and an anticipated increase in traffic due to the coming of the railway, East-the-Water. Old photographs show how unfortunate was the effect of the cast iron parapets and extended steel and iron corbels, surmounted by gas lights. The work was completed by 1867 at a cost of £6,000.

By the end of the century the state of the Bridge, and in particular of the cutwaters, was giving cause for concern, and further widening and strengthening was undertaken in 1925, giving a finished roadway of 16 feet with pavements of seven feet.

The toll house and two chapels are thought to have been demolished some time after 1810.

At one time visitors were intrigued by the notice on the Bridge warning against the removal of mussels. The piers of the Bridge were protected by cutwaters formed from loose stones held in place by basketwork known as sterlings, and the mussels formed an additional protective layer holding the whole thing in place!

During the night of 9th January 1968 the two arches closest to the town cracked. But although the Bridge had obviously to be closed, it showed no signs of collapse and it took a very considerable effort to demolish the carriageway so that repairs could be carried out. The road surface was widened at this western end, and the traffic lights, thought to have been a contributory cause of the cracking through the vibration of traffic, were removed.

The Bridge is scheduled as an Ancient Monument, and has passed to the control of the Ministry of Transport. As well as the main trunk road to Cornwall, it also carries gas, water and electricity, and the transatlantic telephone cable.

Until this time it was owned and administered by the Bridge Trust, a body of 18 prominent Bideford men, known as Feoffees, who have existed almost as long as the Bridge itself, and who over the centuries have acquired a very considerable amount of property in and around the town, the income of which provided the necessary funds for the maintenance of the Bridge.

A beautifully constructed model of the Bridge showing its varying stages of development is on display in the Burton Art Gallery.

It is not known just when the first Bideford quay took shape along the river's edge. The natural progression from the Bridge is along Bideford's Quay, its second most important feature and one from which it derives much of its character. Tree-lined, wide and spacious, it has been called a boulevard with a French air. But the Quay owes nothing to any foreign influence; it grew with the needs of a working port, and a working quay it is still. It is the trees and the distance from the buildings that are largely responsible for its attractiveness, despite the unimaginative placing of the public conveniences, and accumulation of parked cars.

The Quay took on its present appearance at the end of the nineteenth century when it was widened throughout its entire length, resurfaced and the trees planted. In recent years there have been losses, due to Dutch Elm disease and sheer old age, but young replacements should ensure that Bideford's Quay retains its leafy character.

Upstream from the Bridge was completely undeveloped, the riverbank utilised by fishermen and small boatyards. Downstream was a mixture of gardens, warehouses, sheds and small wharves. The earliest quay was believed to run from Conduit Lane – the gardens of the Grenville's town house intervened between it and the Bridge – to the bottom of High Street, and in 1663 this was extended to the area now known as Jubilee (or Landivisiau) Square. Its limits are marked by inscribed paving stones. It was this that became known as Broad Quay and has always been the centre of maritime activities. The Harbour Office is here facing the modern tourist kiosk across the old weighbridge, but today the Square is more often full of articulated lorries unloading supermarket stores than with lorries weighing cargoes loaded from shipping moored across the Quay.

Over the centuries the Quay has been widened and extended several times. In 1692 Broad Quay was found to be inadequate and was extended to the ed of Bridgeland Street, itself a new development. The greatest impact was made when in 1758 the short length connecting the Quay with the western end of the Bridge was constructed.

Early prints and photographs show a narrow, poorly surfaced quay, lined with bollards linked by chains. These were erected as a protection after a series of accidents, the worst of which occurred in 1847 when eight people were drowned, passengers on an omnibus that backed over the edge into the river.

Although the days when the name was justified have now all but passed, Bideford is still distinguished by the title of 'Port'. The town's history is a long one, going back to the Domesday Book when it was recorded as having a fishery, and the town's first charter was granted around 1202 at the instigation of the Grenville family, whose long association with Bideford lasted until 1707. A further charter for a market and fair was granted by Queen Elizabeth I, when the town was made a free borough with powers of self government, rights that are jealously preserved to this day.

The Port flourished as trade with the New World expanded; it is popularly believed in Bideford that England's first cargo of tobacco was unloaded here by Sir Walter Raleigh, and certainly it played an important part in the town's trade.

An account in the Bideford Gazetteer of 1902 describes the town:

In the reign of Charles I the Bideford merchants imported large quantities of wool from Spain, and afterwards besides their commerce with Holland, and France, and the Mediterranean, had so large a share of the Newfoundland trade, that in the year 1699 they sent out more ships than any other port in England, except London and Topsham, the numbers being London 71, Topsham 34, Bideford 28, Bristol 12, Plymouth 5 and Liverpool 3. The chief of the vessels belonging to the port are now employed in the coastal trade. The quay is upwards of 1200 feet in length and at high water vessels of 500 tons burden can discharge their cargoes. Ship-building is carried on to a very considerable extent, and gives employment to many of the inhabitants. Silk-weaving was introduced here in 1650 and after the revocation of the Edict of Nantes, in 1685, many French Protestants settled in the town, and established the manufacture of silk and cotton, but the trade has long since died away.

The decline of Bideford as a port was blamed on a growing preoccupation with the Continent, the European Wars, and growing piracy, mainly by French privateers, that gave to Bideford Bay and the Bristol Channel the nickname of the Golden Coast – not because of the sand but because of the rich pickings to be had from the shipping.

Trade with Maryland and Virginia ceased about 1760 and to America in general some 12 years later. At the end of the century there was a small revival of the American trade with cargoes of timber, pine planks and tar imported from Nova Scotia. At that time the number of vessels registered at the Port was nearly 100, ranging from 250 tons to 20 tons. But Bideford's days as an important port were over. Trade became coastal, with coals and culm from Wales, and oak bark exported to Ireland and Scotland, and the usual trade in agricultural and building supplies.

As the port declined, so did the shipbuilding industry; the two had been inextricably linked, and it was a sad day when the last shipbuilding yard finally closed in 1978. Most of the other yards had

The Town Hall across St Mary's churchyard

closed long before, only a few surviving to the turn of the century.

The buildings at the western end of the Bridge make an imposing group, but are all relatively modern. The red brick Elizabethan-style Town Hall dates from 1850 and replaced an earlier version built around 1698. This building at one time housed the Police Station and cells, one of the town's prisons having been lost along with the original Town Hall. The adjoining library that fronts the river was added in 1906 when the old shops and stabling facing the Bridge were demolished. The substantial late nineteenth century block opposite, described as a 'splendid pile' was originally the new Bridge Hall built by the Bridge Trust, and was considered a great improvement on the mid-eighteenth century Bridge Hall and Grammar School with its open-arched lower storey that had previously occupied the site. Both buildings now house the Torridge District Council.

This development was made possible by the construction of the embankment and roadway in 1827 at the same time and as part of the new valley route to Torrington. Prior to this the road lay East-the-Water and over Gammaton Moor.

Upstream of Bideford Bridge was once a shipbuilding area. One old painting shows vessels of some size under construction but without their masts; these were added downstream after the hulls had been floated through the Bridge.

The embankment replaced a beach and slipways, and it was here that the fishermen of the town kept their boats and tackle. The arches of their fish cellars have long been blocked in, but can still be seen in the wall adjoining the road, underneath the Police Station. It is said that when the Station was built in 1897 the area on which it stands had to be filled in and were considered the cellars of the former nunnery. Te fish cellars opened directly onto the beach, and the pool was known as Nunnery cast. It is still a favourite with the salmon netsmen.

Victoria Park was laid out in the early years of the twentieth century and contains many fine shrubs and trees as well as the usual swings and roundabouts. Built beneath the level of the embankment, it is usually a sheltered spot in which to relax amidst the excellent floral displays.

Surrounding the now rarely used bandstand are the Armada guns. At one time these served as posts on the quayside, but it has been established that they are genuine Spanish guns used by the Armada fleet, presumably brought back to Bideford from a captured Spanish vessel.

Also in the Park is the Burton Art Gallery, named after its donor. This pleasant building houses an interesting collection of local pottery, silver goods, model bone ships made by French prisoners of war, and works by local artists. One very interesting picture, recently restored, is of Bideford

Victoria Park (above)

Kingsley Statue (top right)

The Burton Art Gallery (bottom right)

A tranquil autumn morning

Rotting wooden hulks contrast with the modern bridge

in 1854. It clearly shows the riverbanks and old shipyards and limekilns, and the tramway erected from the riverbank East-the-Water to the Chappel Park anthracite mine.

At the far end of the Quay where now stands the modern Post Office and older Art School, were the old Manor House and the area known as Manor Wharf. The Customs House at the bottom of Bridgeland Street survives, currently as a restaurant and wine bar.

Rope Walk, running behind the Post Office is a relic of Bideford's maritime past. It was down this narrow alleyway and beyond into The Strand that the newly made ropes were stretched around a series of posts, removed when the works closed in 1886.

Kingsley Statue. The monument to the town's great man of letters was erected in 1906 at a cost of over £600, raised by public subscription. It is of white Sicilian marble on a granite base and was surrounded by iron railings. Vandalism is not as new as we are led to believe – within one month

Pottery was once an important trade in the town. Harry Juniper's famous Harvest Jugs, and much else besides, is to be found under the mermaid in Rope Walk

Kingsley had lost the point of his pen. Charles Kingsley spent some of his childhood at Clovelly where his father was Rector. He returned to Bideford in 1854 and rented what is now the Convent School.

In 1855 his novel 'Westward Ho!' was published and Bideford and its environments found themselves the subject of a best seller. It must surely be a rare instance of a new development growing up because of, and being called after, a book, rather than the other way around. Charles Kingsley died on the 23rd January, 1875.

The Strand once fronted the Pill creek, and along the foreshore wharves and small quays lined the banks bringing a maritime flavour into the heart of the town. Architecturally it possesses some fine houses, including the imposing Waterloo terrace.

Bridgeland Street was Bideford's first, and most successful attempt at speculative town development. It was built between 1690 and 1700 on land owned by the Bridge Trust as something

The Strand

of a speculative development to attract the rising wealthy merchant class. Although the righthand side (as you walk up from the Quay) has suffered considerably in the way of shop fronts etc., the lefthand side remains largely as it must always have looked although only one or two are still private residences. Most have generous courtyards and gardens to their rear, and they were a very visible indication of the port's growing prosperity.

Mill Street is much older, and was the original thoroughfare from one end of the town to the other before the Quay became continuous. The uniform shop fronts disguise some very old dwellings, much altered over the years but still identifiable as original Bideford.

The parish church of St Mary was built in 1862, after the original had decayed to such an extent it was considered not worth saving. Only the tower remains of the earlier structure, which in turn was believed to have incorporated the original Saxon church. Its memorials and gravestones commemorate many worthy and interesting Bidefordians, including the one time Mayor, John Strange, who gave his own life inspiring the townsfolk when plague struck in 1646, brought, it is said, from a cargo of Spanish mariner wool. Rawleigh, a Red Indian brought back by Sir Richard Grenville who only survived North Devon's climate for one year, is also recalled by a headstone.

The Church is the centre of a pleasant group of cottages, where the car is banned, and where, as a consequence, there have been virtually no changes since it was first developed.

There was a time when the twice-weekly **pannier market** was in danger of fading away. Fortunately in recent years it has gained a new lease of life, and if not quite so busy as it was in the first half of the twentieth century, then at least it seems set to survive. Covered markets may be rare elsewhere in the country, but are quite common in Devon, where they were established as a place for the farmers' wives to bring their wares, usually carried in panniers by donkeys or packhorses, and sell to the townsfolk. This they still do (though not in panniers) and it gives visitors a rare chance to discover for themselves how much better really fresh produce tastes! The booths, or small shops on the lower terrace, were once almost entirely reserved for butchers, poulterers and the like. Nowadays there is a growing trade in memorabilia, crafts and antiques.

The open floor of the market has in its time been

The Pebble Ridge from Westward Ho!

Downstream from the riverbank walk

used for political rallies, boxing matches, concerts and a variety of other entertainments. The present building dates from 1883 replacing the original old corn market which had become a 'miserable tumbledown structure'.

Old Town, at the top was originally a small collection of cottages, few of which survive. Clovelly Road, the main road up until the opening of the new bridge and bypass, is broad and lined with substantial houses.

The town came to an official end at the old toll house, which operated until 1882. Beyond where once all was green fields and open countryside, the town has spread and spread. Before long it will reach all the way to the new roundabout where the link road comes in.

The High Street is the principal thoroughfare rising up through the town. It gets narrower as it climbs the hill. At one time it contained all the town's important shops, and the most imposing buildings housed the Banks. Currently much of the town is under threat; many shops have closed unable to withstand the financial depression of the latter part of the twentieth century; bustling businesses that have survived for two or three generations have disappeared, and in their place creeps a tide of money-related concerns – building societies, financial advisers, insurance companies and the like. Large chunks remain completely derelict, particularly around the market, and until their future is decided it will be difficult for Bideford to present an attractive face to the world. There is hope, though for some of these are being converted back into homes, thus in one move reviving shut up buildings and bringing people back into the heart of the town. Perhaps the next step will be the revival of small cornershops as people who live in towns are often without the means to visit 'out-of-town' shopping complexes.

An early view of Market Place

Both Bideford and Appledore still hold regattas in the late summer. Rowing was once a very popular sport and competition was fierce. In recent years motorised sports have rather taken over, but both have active rowing clubs, and the annual regattas attract crews from a wide area, though perhaps it doesn't quite live up to the description given in a Bideford guide book of the 1960s.

PORT OF BIDEFORD REGATTA

Bideford Regatta is considered by Bidefordians and visitors to be the great day of the year. It is usually held during the first week in September and is visited by people from far and wide.

The actual Regatta, as a rule, is divided into three parts – one day being set aside for rowing, another for fireworks display and a third for land sports. Regatta Day proper is confined to Rowing: the local competitors are challenged by crews from the whole of the West of England, Bideford's colours being worthily carried by the Amateur Athletic Club and the Amateur Rowing Club, both of whom have been established for many years and whose rowing prowess is renowned in the West. The races are mainly four-oared and pair-oared, rowed in

outrigged shell boats of the best type. The Regatta itself is of very ancient origin, and its earliest records are lost in antiquity.

The river looks its best in Regatta week, animated with the movement and the coloured favours of competing crews, the sailing dinghies, and innumerable small craft of all descriptions, and reflecting the azure sky, and the green of surrounding hills and trees and vivid splashes of colour from the Fair on the Pill.

The firework display presented in the Sports Ground is one of the best of the kind given in the West Country, every effort being made for visitors to see the spectacular items in comfort.

The Sports have a reputation unparalleled in the district, and runners, cyclists and other athletes make special efforts to attend these sports annually. The Cycle events are worth special mention and international riders are frequent competitors.

Regatta Week is closely followed by the Carnival. The old tradition of parading decorated floats around the town is still kept up in many Westcountry towns and villages, culminating with an enormous display of all the winners at Bridgwater in November. Weeks of work goes into the preparation of displays on a wide variety of themes, mostly humorous, and the bystanders reward them by throwing money into the floats.

Estuary and River Life

It was in 1980 that the *Waverley* paid her first visit to the estuary. She has returned every season since and given delight to thousands. For the *SS Waverley* is the last ocean-going paddle steamer, and whilst she spends most of her time in her home waters around the Firth of Forth, the voyage south has become an annual event.

She was launched in 1946, the last paddle steamer to be built on the Clyde, and entered regular service first for the London and North Eastern Railway Co and then as part of Caledonian Macbrayne's fleet. Steamers were an integral part of the transport system of that watery part of the world. Paddle steamers were once a common enough sight on the Bristol Channel providing pleasure cruises up and down the coasts and across to Wales. But with the increase in car ownership and improved road systems, the popularity of this form of travel quickly declined, helped by the reduction in the number of piers along the coasts, as these expensive structures were allowed to deteriorate.

By 1973 Caledonian Macbrayne decided she was no longer an economic proposition and offered the *Waverley* for sale. It was assumed she would be preserved in a maritime museum somewhere, as one of the last surviving 'paddlers'. This was apparently the intention of the Paddle Steamer Preservation Society when they purchased her for one good Scots pound in November 1973. But steam enthusiasts being what they are, talk of museums and preservation soon turned to new engines, boilers, seaworthiness etc. and in much the same way that hordes of people will happily

"SS Waverley"

spend their free time restoring steam railways, there was no shortage of volunteer labour to work on the *Waverley*. In May, 1975, she left dry dock in Glasgow and once more sailed proudly down the Clyde.

So popular have her cruises become that she has now been joined by the *Balmoral,* a steamer but without paddles. If your visit coincides with that of the Clyde steamers, they are an experience not to be missed.

Regular sailings are made from Bideford by the *SS Oldenburg,* the Lundy supply ship. As well as making the 21 mile crossing with passengers and supplies, she also cruises along the North Devon coast.

Northam Burrows is on borrowed time. An old saying prophecies that when the third Charles reigns, the sea will reclaim its own and once more reach to Bone Hill, on the edge of Northam village. From here, the land falls steeply to the flat sandy levels which become the salt marshes of the Burrows, protected only by the ever shifting Pebble Ridge. Few would deny that it is only a question of time before the sea finally breaches the ridge and rushes in.

Over the centuries this natural phenomenon has been on the move.

At one time the Pebble Ridge was more extensive than it is today, and the marsh behind it also, especially at its northern end. Early in the last century, the area of the latter probably exceeded a thousand acres, and the sea is said to be encroaching on the land at the rate of thirty feet a year. Between 1855 and 1861, no less than 87 acres were destroyed. This, in part, has been due to the removal of the pebbles of the ridge for use as "road metal". In recent years a considerable outcry has been raised against this proceeding, and the removal of the pebbles is, we understand now prohibited. It is also believed that the average size of the pebbles was formerly larger than it is today, and that they travelled up from the West in greater quantities than at present.

At the same time the encroachment is probably due, in part at least, to the natural gain of the sea on the land, and were it not that the Burrows are an object of local pride on account of their picturesqueness, and their usefulness for the purposes of golf, probably little attention would have been paid to the matter.

From *Coast Scenery of North Devon* by E A Newell Arber 1911

Between 1872 and 1906 the Ridge was pushed back 400 yards at the Westward Ho! end. From then until 1928 when the new sea defences halted further erosion, there was considerable loss of property.

The original Union Club house was at this end, built prominently close to the Ridge, and had to be abandoned and pulled down in 1879 after several scares when waves and pebbles were dashed against its windows, and the sea finally undermined it.) The terrace of houses that now end at the slipway once extended for almost twice its present length – vanishing one by one into the waves.

In 1957 there was again great concern and it was estimated that the Ridge had receded by at least seven feet over the past eighteen months. Ways and means of stabilising it were again considered, but the Government expressed itself unwilling to contribute to the cost because the ground behind 'was private property'. (Until 1977 the Burrows and much of Appledore and Northam were held on 200 year leases from the Melhuish estate. However, there was no known lessor and on the expiry of the leases most owners considered themselves to be freeholders. That winter the army bulldozers came to the rescue, and spent many hours shovelling pebbles back from the landward side and piling them back onto the Ridge.

The problem of the Ridge has caused much debate. Locals who have lived with the sea and the gales most of their lives hold the view that nature will take its course, and all of man's efforts are puny and ineffective. It is only a question of time, and the best policy is to leave the Ridge alone. After all, as a natural feature it has stood up to the Atlantic for many hundreds of years. However, those with other people's money to spend and much scientific knowledge, have tried to effectively stabilise the shifting pebbles. In 1969 large black wire cages were constructed, filled with pebbles and placed breakwater fashion at intervals along the Ridge. You can still see remains of them poking through the pebbles.

The Burrows – a title that includes all the land behind the Pebble Ridge, is considered by local people to be common ground. 'Potwallopers', as the rate payers are known, have grazing rights and right of free entry, both jealously guarded as was fiercely demonstrated when the County Council decided in 1973, having purchased the freehold from the Melhuish estate for £9,000, to turn it all into a 'Country Park'. The Burrows committee that had for so long managed the affairs to everyone's satisfaction (more or less) found themselves answerable to County Council officials, and a newly appointed Warden. Areas of the dunes were fenced off to stabilise the marram grass and protect nesting birds; a new visitor centre went up – and so did the car parking charges.

The Royal North Devon Golf Club has had its home on the Burrows since 1863 and provides a championship course popular with visitors and locals alike.

It will be seen that the Burrows is a great playground for the whole area, and one of its greatest assets, so it is to be hoped that the sea will not claim it just yet!

The Dunes and saltmarshes support a wide variety of flora and fauna, unique to this kind of terrain. The Braunton Burrows across the water are a much larger version of the same, with towering sand dunes and the long sandy shore of Saunton.

It is said that the use of part of the Burrows as a rubbish dump has done irrepairable damage. The construction of the road, dating from the war years effectively blocked off a large area of the marshes, raising them and stopping the inflow of the tide, so that they dried out. Curlews, lapwings and other species that were once a common sight, are more of a rarity and no longer breed here in large quantities, and the plants that thrive on wet lands were also adversely affected.

The 'dump road' as it is known, is a popular place with many people. It is one of the few places where the carbound can sit and watch the sea, and it is almost unrivalled for birdwatching. Fishermen come here to dig worms, and the dogs of the area love it. A proposal from the County Council to close the road to vehicles caused great consternation and hopefully will never be implemented.

The birds that are regularly seen on the estuary include oystercatchers hugging the tide line, lapwings, golden plovers, all kinds of gulls, waders including the curlew with its long beak and plaintive cry, Brent geese, various kind of tern in the winter months, and varieties of duck. Occasionally a rarity visits the estuary, and then there is great excitement amongst the 'twitchers' who come from all over the country to catch a glimpse of the visitor.

Growing on the dunes that edge the estuary are plentiful clumps of sea holly with its prickly spines, clumps of the beautiful evening primrose and, further inland, drifts of purple flowering thyme and many other unusual plants. Small edible mushrooms are a much sought after delicacy. However, it is best to avoid the large beds of the very aptly named sharp rush that occur throughout the Burrows.

Westward Ho!

The development of Westward Ho! was something new in the history of the area. It is not an enlarged village; there is no nucleus of old or original cottages to be found, no 14th century church tucked away close by a cob and thatch coaching inn, no winding lanes trying to cope with today's lorries and coaches. Westward Ho! was a speculative development dreamed up by a handful of men hoping to bring prosperity to the area, and to themselves. They aimed to capitalise on the long sandy beach and wide sweep of the sea, and when the Earl of Portsmouth laid the foundation stone of the Westward Ho! hotel in 1864, he said it was hoped the new resort would rival Torquay.

The railway had reached Bideford in 1855, thus opening up the area to visitors from all over the country. The growth of Instow as a fashionable holiday resort must have been watched with increasing envy and impatience by the businessmen of Torridgeside. The publication of Charles Kingsley's novel 'Westward Ho!' also in 1855 had increased public awareness of the existence of the area, and its attractions. The book was an instant success and was still popular at the end of the century, by which time it had been reprinted 38 times. And the title of his book was the name chosen for the new development. The company was called the Northam Burrows (North Devon) Hotel and Villa Building Company Limited. Sufficient £10 shares were to be sold to raise the money (around £10,000) to purchase 75 acres of what up till then had been farmland. The first

Westward Ho! pier, about 1870

building, the Westward Ho! hotel, still stands at the foot of the steep hill down into Westward Ho! though now converted into flats. This was the new road built by the company, and the descent is still guarded by the Upper Lodge. The former stables of the Hotel were the substantial range on the left at the bottom of the hill, now redeveloped as private dwellings, after many years of decay and neglect. Many of the company's buildings can still be traced, and it was they who established the road pattern and nature of early Westward Ho!

It was quickly realised that the rough nature of the seas were not suited to delicate ladies, and a swimming pool and changing rooms were built (now housing the amusement arcade and the putting green). There was a large ballroom on the first floor, and it must have been a most attractive venue. The men had to take their chance in the sea, or in the pool formed in the rocks, still there today. The local population, used to narrow streets and low, cramped cottages, must have gazed in wonder as the imposing blocks went up, storey by storey, engendering much the same amazement as today's highrise flats, and towering office blocks. Nothing like this had ever been built before in this corner of North Devon. Originally planned as boarding houses and homes for rent to retired service folk and gentry, despite the efforts of the company, Westward Ho! was never quite as popular as had been hoped.

A guide book written in the early 1900s wondered why, with all its natural advantages, Westward Ho! remained so long in the background.

Even now it does not gain the patronage which such beautiful surroundings merit. Great things were said and hoped of the "settlement". However, things seemed to go contrary. The Kingsley Memorial College did not last; the tide washed away the pier and

The large terrace blocks transform Westward Ho! On the beach, an early attempt at stabilisation of the Pebble Ridge appears to be under way

some houses as well; and now the United Services College (where Rudyard Kipling was educated) has been removed. ...Retired officers form a large proportion of the residents and use the Union Club.

The writer goes on to acknowledge the superiority of the golf links and that the majority of visitors who stayed at Westward Ho! were golfers.

It must have been something of a lifeline to the shareholders and to the local trades people when, in 1874, the United Services College took over the lease of the 'twelve bleak houses by the shore' immortalised by its famous old boy, Rudyard Kipling in 'Stalky & Co.'. The college was basically an academy for the sons of military, naval and colonial gentlemen and was to specialise in the production of officer-material for the forces. This was the first block, nearest to Northam, and after the college moved closer to London in 1904, declined until it was nothing more than an almost derelict collection of bedsits, with a questionmark over its future. Conversion into flats by the Council

saved it.

The most imposing of the 'tower blocks' was formed by joining two terraces with a central chapel and gymnasium block when the Kingsley Memorial College was formed, primarily for the sons of the professional classes. It opened in 1882, but lasted only four years, and again is now divided into flats.

Throughout the area there remain many large – overlarge by today's standards – villas and terraces built in anticipation of the boom that never materialised. Once the wealthy deserted, driven out, it is said, by day-trippers from Bideford, Westward Ho! lost its role. It was never really going to compete with Torquay – the climate in North Devon just isn't up to resort standards. Without the input of wealth the harsh, salt-laden winds caused rapid deterioration, and peeling paint and dilapidated frontages did nothing to help. After the war when people wanted cheap holidays by the seaside Westward Ho! enjoyed a considerable run of prosperity but the price was a rash of cheap development, caravan sites wherever they could be fitted in, and amusement arcades in place of the exclusive clubs and swimming baths. It must have seemed like heaven to those used to city life. You didn't need a car, or much money, to enjoy yourself at Westward Ho! There was a huge holiday camp at the top of the hill, known locally as 'Top Camp' where all the usual facilities were provided, and even here the caravan sites grew up. But it seems that this kind of holiday, too, has all but had its day, forced out by cheap continental holidays, and many of the caravan sites have closed. In their place are new building sites and the current growth area in Westward Ho! is in providing retirement homes.

As the visitor walks along the promenade – a rare feature on the North Devon coast, beyond the original Bath House and the later Nassau baths built for the USC college, he may well wonder at the short row of iron stumps exposed by the receding tide. This is all that is left of the ambitious proposal to build a pier – without which no

Westward Ho! from across the Burrows

An early postcard view of Westward Ho!

The riverbank

Bright flowers above the RNLI boathouse

Victorian seaside resort was complete. Work began in 1870, but the original 600 foot length was always overambitious, and a severe gale in the autumn of 1870 caused so much damage that only the first 150 feet was salvaged. It is a great shame that the attractive little structure did not survive as it would have been much appreciated today, but more storms in 1880 sealed its fate, and the iron structure was dismantled.

Another lost feature that would have been immensely popular was the Bideford to Westward Ho! railway. The craze for laying tracks was such that many outlandish schemes were proposed. However, this one was actually built and the first trains ran in 1901. To reach Westward Ho! the line went in a huge loop away from the estuary towards Abbotsham and back again along the coast to Westward Ho! and later on to Appledore. There had been a plan to build a form of barrage across the estuary and take the line directly from Instow to Appledore, but this was thought impractical. As a tourist attraction it would have ranked with the best; as a sensible method of getting around it was a non-starter. It was both quicker and cheaper to travel from Bideford to Northam and Westward Ho! by horsedrawn bus. The line, which actually ran along the Quay at Bideford, eventually went to support the war effort in 1917. The level track bed forms a popular walk along the cliffs towards Cornborough and Abbotsham.

Lifeboat History

If ever a stretch of coast was in need of a rescue organisation, it was North Devon. Even the waters of Bideford Bay did not provide safe shelter if the wind was in the wrong direction, and vessels were carried steadily and mercilessly towards the rocky shore. The sea bed must be littered with the debris of wrecks, if you but knew where to look. Rusting metalwork is not so common, as ships were less vulnerable once they had engines to rely on. Even so, the coast has claimed a few since the days of sail, the last being the *Eva V* off Abbotsham in 1981.

Appledore was one of the earliest stations to receive a lifeboat in February 1825. The *Volunteer* was 17 feet long, and was powered only by four or five men, rowing. It seems unbelievable today that men should put to sea in a rowing boat to rescue people they knew nothing about, risking their own lives in the process. Yet the Appledore crew did just that, time and time again.

The second lifeboat came in 1831, the *Assistance*, and was a more substantial 26 footer, with six oars. She saved 27 lives over 17 years, for the loss of three crew drowned in 1833 when the *Assistance* capsized. The *Volunteer* launched and saved the crew and the *Assistance*. She was a supplementary boat to the *Volunteer* which simply was not man enough to reach some of the vessels in distress. The first lifeboat house was built at Watertown to house both vessels.

The *Assistance* was replaced by the *Petrel*, 28 feet long with 10 oars and costing £125, which was raised locally. But she was not successful and was replaced in 1852. The second *Petrel* was stationed on Northam Burrows where the RNLI was to have its headquarters for 37 years. From 1824 to 1831 the Appledore Station was run by the Bideford Committee, the North Devon Humane Society taking over in that year, but in 1855 it officially became a part of the RNLI. The following year it was decided that the *Volunteer* had finally had her day. In her 31 years of service she had saved 88 lives – one wonders what became of her.

Next time you are sitting on the Pebble Ridge watching the huge Atlantic breakers crashing on the shore, imagine how it must have felt to launch the lifeboat into that thundering surf, and row out through it to the rescue of a vessel in danger in the bay. Cart horses were used to drag the lifeboat from her boathouse on the far end of the Burrows (where Lifeboat Green is aptly named on the golf course). By keeping her here in preference to the original boathouse at Appledore, the crew were saved the additional hazard of crossing the Bar, and were not so badly affected by the tide – though it must have been a long haul across the soft sands if the alarm went off at low tide.

In 1848 a further lifeboat station was built across the estuary at Braunton – although the crew still had to row across from Appledore. The two stations ran in tandem until it was decided once again to reopen Appledore in 1889 when the present boathouse was built at Badsteps. Braunton closed down at the end of the first World War after a losing battle to keep going when most of the horses and able-bodied men had been draughted to the Front. Appledore had a slip, so that horsepower was no longer essential. It was not until 1922 that the first motorised lifeboat in the Bristol Channel arrived, and since 1938 the lifeboat has been moored permanently in Appledore Pool.

The nature of the work of the RNLI has changed considerably since the end of the Second World War. The need for a lifeboat service arose to protect and rescue the large numbers of small coasters that plied their trade, slipping from port to port, and of the fishermen who put to sea in small craft in all weathers – all of them relying on their skill and knowledge as seamen to get them out of difficulties in those days of sail. Coasters are almost a thing of the past, and the fishing fleets are going the same way. Those who crewed the lifeboats similarly relied on their own knowledge and strength and bravery to rescue their fellow seamen. Today they are no less courageous – but a knowledge of electronics is useful! There has never been, and never will be, a shortage of men and women volunteering to risk their lives to save others – and no shortage of the back up teams raising funds and organising lifeboat days for the enjoyment of holidaymaker and local alike.

In recent times a completely new need arose – the estuary and coast has become increasingly popular with swimmers, surfers, sailboarders, windsurfers etc all of whom have been known to get into difficulties. To answer this new need, Appledore acquired an *Atlantic 21* inshore lifeboat – designed along the lines of a large inflatable with very shallow draught, and able to skim across the waves at any state of the tide. This first boat was placed at Appledore on evaluation trials in 1972-73-74 – which proved an outstanding success, and in 1975 the first permanent inflatable arrived.

It is a grand record to look back on and one of which Appledore folk are justly proud. Since the first lifeboat arrived in 1825, 753 (to the end of 1994) lives have been saved with the loss of three lifeboatmen. Twenty lifeboats and three Inshore Lifeboats have achieved this and the crews have been awarded 22 silver and six bronze and four Foreign medals.

The lifeboathouse at the west end of Appledore, now houses the inshore boat and the launching tractor, both kept in that pristine condition that makes one wonder if they ever get wet and muddy. There is also a gift stall, and many fascinating photographs and memorabilia around the walls, and visitors are welcome. The lifeboat *George Gibson* is permanently at her moorings in Appledore Pool.

Regatta Day at Appledore